my father's gloves

by david spiering

Flat Sole Studio
St. Paul, Minnesota

Published by Sol Books,
an imprint of Flat Sole Studio,
https://flatsolestudio.com

Copyright © 2010 Flat Sole Studio

All rights reserved. No part of this publication
may be reproduced in whole or in part
without written permission of the publisher.

Acknowledgements
The author and publisher wish to express their grateful appreciation to the following publications in which earlier versions of these poems first appeared: "Country Music: A Lament", *Nanny Fanny*; "Fast-talking Pol Searches for the World's Tiger Tail", *The Writers Journal*; "German Lessons", *Red Owl Review*; "Johann Strauss: The Younger", *The Rockford Review*; "My Father & Dylan Thomas", *The Wabash Review.*

Library of Congress Cataloging-in-Publication Data:
Spiering, David.
    My Father's Gloves: Poems / by David Spiering.
    p. cm. – (Sol Books Upper Midwest Writers Series)
    ISBN 978-0-9793081-6-1 (pbk.)
    ISBN 978-0-9793081-8-5 (e-book)
    I. Title.
PS3619.P5437A88 2010
811'.6—dc22   2008032396

Credits:
Blake Hoena, editorial direction
Donald Lemke, cover design
Flat Sole Studio, book layout

Summary: *My Father's Gloves* touches on that most conflicted of family bonds, the one between fathers and sons. With a hauntingly painful voice, Spiering explores the burdensome yoke of a father's expectations and the struggles a son must face as he grows into manhood. His poems are accessible and wrought with emotions, his descriptions subtle in their complexity, his pace slow and deliberate.

Contents

My Father's Gloves 7

Family Poems, an Outside View
Imaginary Conversation with My Uncle 11
Marriage and Family 12
Johann Strauss: The Younger 13
Tackle Box Memorial 14
Bad Fathers 15

Father and Mother Poems, an Image Portrait
Father Figure 19
There's Nothing He Can Do Now 20
My Father & Dylan Thomas 21
I Never Think of My Father as Young 22
Disjunction 23
An Intuitive Master Lesson 24
Zippo Lighter 25
My Father's Lessons about Thrift 26
Pears 28
German Lessons 29
Memories of Mermaid Ave. 18: All the Marbles
    Squeezed in My Palm 32
Another Thing I'm Glad for when I Think of
    My Father 33

A Cracked View Through the Angled Pale
Fast-talking Pol Searches for the World's
   Tiger Tail 37
Country Music: A Lament 38
To a Cigarette Smoker Standing Outside the
   Coffee Shop 39
My Purpose Is to Elevate 40
Eastward Sketchers 41
Dolefulness 42
Without Tears 43

Great Lakes Sequence
Arctic Cold [A True Romance] 47
Doubt 48
Moments, Outright Happy 49
An Exhumed Pulse Meant as Movement 50
Venus Says 51
A Boat Ride in a Northern River in
   Late Spring 52
That's Hard to Say 53

My Father's Gloves

I wonder if his hands are still
crossed in the coffin
after ten years dead; a second
dead is as good as a million years –
snuff out the stars;
I wear his leather dress gloves
everyday as I walk through the freezing
rain, carrying my ancestor's
cells in my fingertips,
in my groin and beneath my toenails,
but my life has wrinkled the gloves
that his pensiveness kept new;
I own them for one week and they're rumpled
from rough use – my bear-rolling hills,
risk taking and searching out the sky's
ladder that I know is there to find.

Family Poems,
an Outside View

Imaginary Conversations with My Uncle

"I hate Roy Orbison," my uncle says,
"he sings like he has a belly ache after
eating a dozen green apples." I don't
want to give into his verbal bantering;
I let my Orbison CD spin in my clear blue-tinted
clamshell shaped player – Roy's black glasses
and hair spun into black circular bands.
"He's too emotingly emotional," my uncle says.
"What about opera?" I say.
"Now that's true passion – time tested and hand hammered."
"I think opera's too falsely sentimental – I do – but I
like overtures – but when those tenors
and sopranos begin their screeing it makes my
skin roll sleeve-like on my bones," I say.
"You don't know true good music," he says.
I saw this was going into a vicious circle
argument where two people lock arms and go
around and around with no hope of resolution
or understanding; I put on my headphones,
and the music drowns out my uncle's voice.

Marriage and Family

My family is Lutheran and when
my grandmother died my aunt (who
married a Roman Catholic but remained
a Lutheran and her children were
raised as Catholics – something
that didn't sit well with the family)
my aunt told me that when she was in Germany
there were nuns and confessional booths
in the Lutheran churches she saw.
I asked my sister about this, "why
would our aunt say this to me?"
and my sister answered, "because she's
married to a Roman Catholic."
Okay, I thought and poured
milk over my grain-made cereal-Os.

Johann Strauss: The Younger

My German grandmother played 78s
of Strauss, and the music soaked into my blood,
built structures in my ways of thinking,
made roads I travel to clouds,

made threads of feeling and understanding.
I tangle through the planets –

                              punk

rock couldn't thrash it out;
the Rolling Stones gathered its mossy
fleecing and lodged in the tall grass; jazz
couldn't cool it or bebop into
my periphery – I crawl

farther into the sound texture,
but I can't touch its root sources.
The music forms my body and intellect
into a ball and rolls me over its textures.

Tackle Box Memorial

I open my tackle box and view all the bright shining baits;
I've had them for years and I'm afraid to fish
with them because they can't be replaced if I snag them
on a sunken log or in the mangroves; besides, throughout
the years many of them were given to me as gifts
to help me build my collection; the plugs I bought
myself look like newly hatched fish down to skin
texture and they hum and rattle to attract fish
when retrieved; the silver-bright spoons
were given to me by my long deceased neighbor;
my Rapala cost me a week's worth of tips
from my paper route; I have Swedish and Danish jigs my
    uncles
gave me that I coffin as memorials to them, besides
that, they're collector's items; I think how my grandfather
fished with ham fat and dough balls; when I fish
now I use cheap terminal tackle; if I lose
one I have many to replace it; it's like dropping
a memoric gold nugget into the water; it's seemingly
lost and gone forever.

Bad Fathers

If I could name the bad
children's fathers, selling deceit

with smiles, having consciences filled with

tales of personal failure, their only

sense of gain centered on destroying
people's attempts at

happiness, I'd call their fathers my weariness

to sort truth's detail's dark strands
from less truthful shades.

Father and Mother Poems, an Image Portrait

Father Figure

I saw my father standing
outside the bus station

with his life jumbled
and knotted in nylon duffel

bags; I pass him thinking
how he was similar

to the wind flicking rain
from its hands; after

he passes from my sight,
I search for the figurative

father, giving council
unprejudiced by nature

or other concerns,
a father I observe

kneading out his dreams'
kinks, using the skill

of his cunning to graft
them toward fruition.

There's Nothing He Can Do Now

September catches me
in my father's fields – I
began this fatal longing
dizzy with love and injustice I
cannot return from –
even when my stomach
hangs between my knees,
my conscience gables
the arrival of what
tomorrow brings – I
smile at shadows
moving behind me
and into me, my fingertips
are candle flames
pouring light
through narrow slates.

David Spiering

My Father & Dylan Thomas

As a teenager
I paged through
Time Magazine
coming to a photo

of Dylan Thomas
rail sitting
at the White Horse
Tavern. I said

to my father,
"who's Dylan Thomas?"
he said, "a bad
man and a drunk."

I went to the library
to learn about
Dylan Thomas; after
reading poems, journals,

notebooks and a biography,
I told my father
I wanted to be
just like Dylan Thomas.

I Never Think of My Father as Young

I turn myself
around and
around, trying to dry
all the impressions, blots
and stains my father
made on me; as I turn, I imagine
how my father was
still a young man when
he was 150 years old; he looked
like a child in a photo
of a pioneer family I saw at a museum;
my father was 250 years old
when I was born; in this
photo his face reflects
all the back peddling, all
the larger crows and bluejays
driving him from tree to tree –
he didn't know how to
make sense of it; he just flew
and it made him older and older yet –
then and now my father hovers
half-blind to his history lessons,
fading as shadows at noon.

Disjunction

I saw my father
wearing the sod breeches
my mother and sisters
preferred for him that day

a hole in the sky
took me to where
he lived since his
death

he didn't say
much to me

then a rain torrent
sprayed hose-like
on his front window

he looked at me
with his worried
hurried expression,
(the one I remembered
from when he lived)
as if he were already
tired of my company

he said to me,
"how am I going
to get you home?"

An Intuitive Master Lesson

my dad was a jacket,
a tie and a pair
of Wall Street creased
pants and leather dress
shoes that never showed any wear
but no star was his, he
never eternalized light –
the trees' shadows
swallowed his words,
he attended the school of salts
and pounded salt all his life
but he acted like he had the ultimate
fire formula while keeping
his eyes fixed seaward

he never understood my desire
to swim; he wanted me to cleave
to money and stone and avoid
unforgivable ocean torrents

I tried for stone and money, but
I wasn't happy, my heart's violets
were torn up, I came to my senses
pulling my hair out by the handful
while I splashed in the ocean waves.

Zippo Lighter

my father was a heavy cigarette smoker –
his lungs and his blood were sealed and saturated
with smoke – he told
me it was okay to pipe and cigar puff, but stay
away from cigarettes, he said "look what they've
done to me," he said – he had breathing issues
and he couldn't climb steps;

as I forage through my man-purse (my backpack) I
find my father's old Zippo lighter circa the 1950s,
his initials scribed on it –

after I showed the lighter to my mother, she told me that
    before I
was born, the family watched the 4th of July
fireworks in a city park waterfront reclined on a blanket,
    his lighter
fell out of his pocket – after they were at the car
my father wanted to smoke and he realized the lighter
was gone, and he and my mother searched the dark grass
    (on hands and knees)
for almost two hours before they found the lighter

no worries – now – at least no one will have to search a
    long time to find it.

My Father's Lessons about Thrift

Recently, I bought a pack of cheap safety razors

my head filled with my
father's voice-echoes
from my childhood,
angry and pleading at me
as we stood in the hardware
store; I wanted an automatic key ring
retriever like the one Billy
the janitor had
"it cost $3.95,"
my father said,
"that's four bucks;
that's too expensive,"
and he refused to buy it;
there was another option,
a key ring that attached
to a leather belt snap
costing $1.29; because
money was always an issue
I had to settle
for the cheaper option;

I should've understood those
cheap razors would chafe
my cheeks
chin and neck but
they were "cheap"

I went back and bought the pricey
shave-smooth (smooth as running
my fingers on wet tile) – I
should have
bought them the first time
and saved the money
to plunk like pennies
on my father's dead eyes.

Pears

the grocery store piles pears in drab modes –
their charm is the associative
harmony of their collective shapes –
humor leaks from their figures, their stems
jaunt odd angles; their wide bottoms are unafraid
to face up

I consider how
my mother couldn't resist pears; if they
needed ripening she arranged them
to sun on the kitchen windowsill

as a small child I stood
at my mother's elbow while
she peeled a pear; the peelings made
unsonorous plunk, plat, plunk, plunk
in the metal sink –
she cut the pear in half, spooned
out the middle, put
in a large dollop of cottage cheese
and placed it before me; I always
tried to spoon-edge it;
it flipped, spilling the cheese;

I stand in the produce section
peering at the pears; if I bought
some they'd languish on my windowsill
soaking sunshine as vegetables overshadowed them –
perhaps I'd still eat them if they
had not flipped when I tried to slice them.

German Lessons
lesson 1

most mornings before school, I had
breakfast at my grandmother's house and her
friend from our German Lutheran Church joined us – I
hunched over fried potatoes and two bread dough
scraps fried and brown sugar coated – the women
conversed in German; I glanced up and inquired –
my grandmother told me to "keep still" later I
said "what can't you teach me the father
tongue?" her response to my request was,
"maybe someday you'll visit Germany."
she did teach cultural values without
realizing it through the food she prepared: sauerkraut,
potatoes, pork, red cabbage, sauerbraten,
pumpernickel bread, cheese, dumplings and soltz.

lesson 2

I was raised in the absolutist tradition of some Lutheran
    churches
in America – the Pastor thought all the Papists were
    heathens
because they worshiped father, mother, son, saints and
    ghost –
he guarded these theological positions with the bewitched
snarling charm of a rottweiler – as a 15 year old I
ate the Pastor's goulash without separating overall
taste from the preparation method.

lesson 3

my parents battled over the supremacy
of their nationality's literature (my father's
German and my mother's Anglo-Celtic) I
was the benefactor of those clashes, I
read Grass, Heine, Schiller, Goethe, Brecht –
if their clashes caused them turmoil
the good meant my enrichment

synthesis: these lessons effected me – I
eat some German food each week, I
read literature in translation; I hear funny
voices in my head whenever I see a priest –
beyond my behest, these are my cultural
heritage lessons that I'm too deeply
rooted in to give a greater explanation.

Memories of Mermaid Ave. 18: All the Marbles Squeezed in my Palm

my father long dead
approached
me (as I rolled along
on my mountain bike)
in a yellow classic
Camero with blue California
plates; he looked
at me as if snot
ranted in streams
over my mouth – I
wasn't dismayed
by his disapproving looks
because I tuned my back
on his notions
of living life while
he still lived

I put my chin close to the handle bars
as I continued moving forward

Another Thing I'm Glad for when I Think about My Father

at night my folded arms
make a nest for my head
as I look at my new shoes or
stare at my winter-flab belly

thinking how I need to loose 25 pounds;

I think about the morning after and my father
who smoked cigarettes – he filled many rooms
with thick smoke; he
quit and died anyway – I

keep looking at my new dress shoes
glad I never smoked cigarettes.

A Cracked View
Through the Angled Pale

Fast-talking Pol Searches for the World's Tiger Tail

he wore green football jerseys;
he shouted at his mother how he's
going to fight the world and win;
his mother yelled back, "they're
going to smother you;" he said, "I'm
tough, I say, I'm tough; "she said,
"you don't have hips to fill the pants
you want to wear;" he had to talk
fast, there was no other way to dodge
stigmatization's sharp screw threads
that people put at him;
he was poor, his father was in jail
for the long term; those were the things
people saw when they looked at him;
the constant abrasions frustrated him,
then enraged him; the rage
deepened into confusion and then
came the house breaking, armed
robbery and arson and the waver
into adult court and a twenty year prison term.

Country Music: A Lament

"if you like pumpkin you'll like squash"
—My father

country music is squash; the twanging
taste whiskey torrents will not blot
out; the plastic mannequin faces
looking as if they've never known
the hard scrabble they sing about
        I'll take the pumpkin in folk
        and blue grass as authentic
        country music; it follows
        the human heart's runnels
        through sand, dirt and filth;
the honesty keeps my blood warm;
                keeps an odorous curtain
                high as wainscoting;
                it feels lived in as sweat stains
                on my mattress;
                as sock holes my toes navigate; as
                the wincing alcohol taste in cheap wine;
                as the bourbon twist cutting each
                organ it touches while coursing my body

To a Cigarette Smoker Standing Outside the Coffee Shop

I'm glad
smoke
never made
my lungs
into a
crow's wings

I watch
the smoker
lean and
cough

there's nothing
to give
him that
won't strike
his eardrums
like unwanted
salt pellets

My Purpose Is to Elevate

I eat God each time
I have pasta –
his blood's the tomatoes,
his bones are the pasta,
his humanity's the great
herbs, basil and oregano
dressed in olive oil
and balsamic vinegar –
yet I can't do as I am
without anyone trying to help
me – Buddha's
a candle burning down
to nothing – I heard something;
perhaps
wind for my sails, a bill
collector taking my phone
off its hook, making me
feel like my bones
are relics to my age

Eastward Sketchers

she saw her father split
the guitar in half –
he did it because
her auntie sat inside
the sound hole
like an echo-mouse –
each time he played
the aunt criticized his heart's
most dear and spontaneous
musings – she told him
he was sinful,
and he needed God
to clean him up –
she tried to keep
him chained to orange-
colored coffee and reminded
him constantly
how God was somewhere
behind the sky
controlling people like
marioncttcs – after he
split the guitar,
she watched her father load it
piece by piece
in a large well drawn
fire in the fireplace –
as it burned, she
watched a dark shadow
approach him from
behind

Dolefulness

my underwear caught on my toes – I can't
jiggle them free – I put a postage stamp on the envelope's
left corner – I
peel it off, replacing it on the right –
papers fall from my hands to the floor – I
keep dropping the soap in the shower –
the leather uppers ripped on my favorite
shoes, but they're still comfortable to me – I toss
a crumbled up paper piece
at the garbage can –
it missed and rolled under a chair –
humidity wraps
around me, and I wonder where I'm
going to look for solace.

Without Tears

the lake's drenched by memory's
weight,
the water's colder than I like –
so, it's another trip to the liquor
store for more beer –
a skunk waddles in the alley
near some garbage cans
my soul's white, black & blue –
I hear voices from
my distant past
telling me, "careful,
careful," on this unfortunate
soil –
when it hurt
I had to cry without tears
because the boat never
touched the shore again
despite the lanterns
held in well-meaning hands
and prayers from those
only imagining how thorns
hurt – but the real lesson
fell apart in their hands
like a wet maple leaf

Great Lakes Sequence

Arctic Cold (A True Romance)

a woman places stones
where it's forbidden

I fix my eyes on a path –
subzero cold covers us

like a skull – the harsh
frozen snow, glass-like

to touch makes her assemble
her little facets into one warmth

she daydreams (in the cold) how
the social heat makes things

and corrupts people's centers
she'll realize then that each-to-each means

the both of us, a will
with our names on it – she

hangs cotton puff-like in my sky
I (my face window framed) look out, waiting

Doubt

we
live
like
our
lives
are
bridges
to the
immortality
of
grass
but
our
lives
hang
like a
light-
weight
summer
shirt
on
a
thin
wire
hanger
subjugated
to
the
wind

Moments, Outright Happy

a sort of sketch —
a body that becomes
stars and starred
as words in my hands
make a report
with delicate tensions — I

watch as a leaf eats
the wind, I think
about snowflake
faces forming
a bland throng
around me —
my blankets smell
like leaf mold
as the night
passes overhead

An Exhumed Pulse Meant as Movement

thick-witted people couple up
while I sit at home drinking beer
and cooking my supper – my hands
have known many secrets my
mouth hasn't the nerve to tell;
I stand in the night-shaded foliage
thinking about cold beer caches
me and I notice how the ground
looks like a moist skull; my diction
swings from my outer edges
in at my soft middle; for
pleasure I run south, my
pelvis feels like it's a stone crock
my legs cut out from my bottom;
my eyes long to gleam at
a blueberry palace slashed
and dumped as punishment
because what had began
to feel like reverence became
a sense of intimate revenge.

Venus Says . . .

[you] looking over
the spellbound classes –
no one messes
with a recognized voice

you believe onions are clever
and angels are islands
with bows and spears for wings –

light seeps around the edges
fog and air fill your open mouths

you crawl into black tornadoes
to battle with your body

you're too anxious to sleep or dream –

everywhere a wagon opera
awakens another child inside you

A Boat Ride in Northern River in Late Spring

is a sketch idea sorted
by dance and stars –

in my hand I hold
my fist, a ticklish report
with tension inside it –

a bug sits on a leaf
as I watch it eat where
it sits

my mind's youthfully bewitched
lodging on morbid beauty
that seems everywhere like smells –

the grass is a blanket –

happiness is an outright moment
discharging its duty
flowing water-like or pointing
to (otherwise) nothing

That's Hard to Say

a ringing phone
drops on a table
like an ashtray – I think
how I drove something new
happy as a poem arrowed
into my father's last chance –
I carry bronze
to dinner with me beneath
my blue coat – a greedy fool
thought it was gold and tried
to tell me it was worthless
as lead; I said I have
the girl I want; when she crossed
her heart
you were nowhere to be seen.

About David Spiering

David Spiering (1961–2020) received his Master of Fine Arts degree in creative writing from Bowling Green, Ohio. His work has appeared in *Chiron Review, The Mid-American Poetry Review, Spillway, The Wisconsin Academy Reivew,* and many other literary reviews and journals.

Spiering has published several chapbooks, including *Crooked Litanies. My Father's Gloves* was his first full-length collection of poetry.

www.ingramcontent.com/pod-product-compliance
Lightning Source LLC
LaVergne TN
LVHW041715060526
838201LV00043B/750